THE LEADER'S JOURNEY

The Leader's Journey

First Edition

"Leadership is the art of giving people a platform for spreading ideas that work."

— Seth Godin, Tribes: We Need You to Lead Us

PART 1

"Leaders aren't born; they are made. They are made just like anything else, through hard work. That's the price we'll have to pay to achieve that goal or any goal."

-Vince Lombardi

WHAT IS THIS BOOK ABOUT?

How do you define leadership? Chances are, if you look back on your career, you could name a few people who you thought were great leaders and made an impact on you in some way. Leadership is a very personal experience, but there are common traits associated with those we deem as "great." If you are reading this book, you are looking for insight into those traits to understand better leadership and how to build those skills for yourself.

Anyone can be a leader. It isn't necessarily about a title or a job description, but it is something that can be learned and developed over time. Leadership is not an easy path. All of us have all known plenty of bad "leaders." Rather it is a journey, a daily practice to be your most authentic self and to create a path to go from where you are to where you want to be both in life and career.

As you go through this book, I ask that you be mindful of the most fundamental aspect of leadership. Remember that leaders are only leaders if people are willing to follow them. There is a huge difference between a manager and a leader. Managers complete tasks as instructed. They generally have a narrow focus on the day-to-day and, far too often, the status quo. Leaders look beyond the current state of things and see what could be. They drive people and organizations forward, far beyond where they thought they could go. Leadership is a calling, a skill, and a practice.

Leadership is desperately needed and sorely lacking. Whether you feel ready or not, you have the potential and the ability to be the leader we all need. This book is about the journey to become a more effective leader, regardless of your job title, organization, or salary. It is about embracing and practicing the qualities of effective leaders that we have all experienced firsthand or read about.

This is a short book, and that is by design. It is not meant to be a textbook but rather a guidebook. As you go through this book, write in the margins, highlight pages, write notes, whatever you need. This is about you and your personal journey to define and craft your leadership style and skills. The journey starts now.

LEADERSHIP MATTERS

Without true leadership, teams and companies become ineffective. We all know there is a void in modern leadership, but what can be done about it? Leadership is an underappreciated resource until it is missing. Leadership is an intangible quality that is noticeable when it is present and even more noticeable when it is absent.

Companies can blame market conditions and the economy all they want to explain their lack of performance. Some of that may be true, but the reality is that it stems from poor leadership combined with poor execution. This leads to underperforming teams and eventually underperforming organizations. Leadership is not something that can be missing for long. There are many examples of successful companies that have gone into the ditch due to poor leadership. Think Apple in the early nineties, before Steve Jobs returned, or GE following Welch's retirement, or Ford prior to Alan Mulally, to name only a few examples.

There is tremendous opportunity here because anyone can be a leader. You can be a leader. It doesn't matter what your role is or what job title you have. Use the mountain of experience, knowledge, and skill that you already possess to be a leader on your team, organization, or community. Be willing to make the hard choices and be able to live with the results. Grow and learn from every experience and from everyone you meet.

BUT WHY?

Without leadership, we get stuck. We get stuck into thinking that what we have in front of us is all that matters or all that could be. Leadership is what drives people and organizations forward. It is about looking around the corner, encouraging people to try something new, learn from risks, or simply see things from a new perspective.

Without leadership, big things just don't get done. Sure, luck, education, and timing play a role but alone cannot move the needle. Leadership is required to motivate and align a large effort or seize an opportunity or build sustainable growth in an organization.

WITHOUT LEADERSHIP, THERE IS A VOID

"Be the yard stick of quality. Some people are not used to an environment where excellence is expected."

- Steve Jobs

Earlier I wrote about a leadership void, but what do I mean by that? Put simply, and it is a lack of genuine leaders who act with vision and determination regardless of what people think of them or what is popular. They do what needs to be done to reach their goals. It is not about what an analyst thinks or what is trendy, but rather to progressively move toward a worthy ideal.

Think about Dwight D. Eisenhower, Henry Ford, Steve Jobs, John D. Rockefeller, J.P. Morgan, Franklin Roosevelt, Winston Churchill, Bill Gates, and many others. History is filled with people who stepped up when needed and took care of business when their company, country, or world needed them the most.

Regardless of what you may think of the people listed above, you cannot deny their ability to lead, drive effective change, change the world, and unite people toward a common goal.

Unfortunately, as this book is being written, we are in a period where that doesn't happen. Our politicians govern via sound bites rather than through sound policy. They try to one up each other or send Twitter blasts to appeal to the lowest common denominator rather than tackle hard problems head-on. Business leaders fail to provide a clear strategic vision and then jump ship when the going gets tough. Employees feel uninspired at best and easily replaceable resources at worse.

Rather than preserving the status quo, we should be using technology and increased connectivity to set big goals and transform the world as we have done many times in the past. The secret of big goals is it energizes people and can empower them to do great things. It encourages them to think big and contribute beyond their everyday job duties. A great leader can turn average into extraordinary.

Unfortunately, instead of big swings to improve society or add shareholder value, we live with small, easily achievable goals. Nothing too big or controversial. Today's so-called leaders live for the next quarter or the next news cycle. Companies are full of disengaged employees who are waiting for the next layoff or reduction in benefits. We have no cause, no big rock to move, and as a result, people grow complacent and comfortable with the status quo.

It is time for that to change.

It is time for people need to wake up, come back to the real world, and demand personal excellence to live an extraordinary life. It is time we demand the same from our leaders, and if they cannot deliver that consistently we need to replace them. Let's stop treating the symptoms of poor leadership and focus on the root cause...tolerance of poor leadership.

You don't have to be a politician or a CEO to be a leader. Leadership starts with you, right now, wherever you are. Seize the moment; take advantage of the opportunity to bring out the best in yourself, in others, and in the world. The world needs leadership more now than ever before.

Will you be that leader?

WHAT DOES IT MEAN TO LEAD TRULY?

Think bold, be a corner bender. Look beyond the everyday tasks and routine of your job, your company, or your life. Think of it like railroad tracks. Managers take care of making sure everything works and the trains run on time. Leaders shift them, change the boundaries, and redefine objectives, strategies, and sometimes limitations.

A leader's thought process must be different. It must be audacious, bold, and bigger than the here and now. It must be forward-thinking, ambitious, engaging, and empowering. You must feel a connection to it. It is inspiring.

To be an effective leader, it is not just about being ten steps ahead of everyone else; and it is about anticipating challenges, obstacles, and opportunities. More importantly, it is about motivating and inspiring your team to move the big rocks, to transform the way they work or the business they are in. It is about empowering your team to execute the strategy for today while tomorrow comes into focus.

WHAT IS THE LEADER'S JOURNEY?

Leadership is a very personal experience, whether as a leader or as a follower. Very few people are natural-born leaders. Most need to develop the skill over time through education, observation, mentors, and personal experience. Just like our careers, leadership evolves over time. If we go beyond the routine, we will continue to grow, learn, and mature. If we apply those experiences to our leadership toolkit, we will improve over time.

Have you ever trained to run a marathon? What about a 5K? If you don't run regularly, you can't just throw on some shoes, run a race, and expect success. However, if you train and practice daily, you get better, building endurance to reach that goal. The same applies to leadership. It is not all or nothing pursuit, nor is it linked solely to your title. Titles can and will change. This is about preparation, refinement, and skill-building.

The leader's journey is a quest, a daily practice to become not only your best self but to inspire others to become their best. It is the connection from where we are today to where we want to be tomorrow. There are common traits associated with great leaders. This is about the journey to uncover those traits, deconstruct them and further develop your own skills.

IT IS INTERNAL

If you think about your career, what made someone a good leader? We all have different opinions on this, but it starts somewhere inside of us. There is a small, still, voice that forces us to volunteer when no one else will or help a co-worker who needs us or be empathic to others. These are all leadership qualities, but they are intangible. They start inside every one of us, and it's just that most people ignore the call or avoid the challenge. Will that be you, or will you rise to meet the challenge and the discomfort of growth?

IT IS PERSONAL

Leadership is a personal experience. From the time we are kids, we encounter people of authority, both good and bad. Sometimes we learn more from the bad than from the good if for nothing other than we don't want to act as they do.

Here are a few simple rules as you think about your leadership journey:

Treat people how you want to be treated.

Think about things from the other person's perspective.

Understand the bigger picture.

How do you define leadership?

Chances are, if you look back at your life and career, you will find someone that made an impact on you. What made you like them? What did they do to make you emulate or remember them? What traits did you admire?

IT IS UNIQUE TO YOU, YET UNIVERSAL TO ALL

This is your journey and your practice. It will not be like mine or anyone else's.

It is yours.

However, take comfort in knowing that there are millions of people, just like you, that are dealing with the same doubt, the same challenges, and the same fears, all the while trying to make themselves better.

Their journey is unique, just like yours, yet all leaders face similar obstacles. It is the approach and the outcome that vary from person to person. Your journey will be unique to you, but others are comrades in arms sharing similar struggles.

IT IS MENTAL

No, it's not just in your head. Bad leadership or a leadership void can and will impact your performance and even your motivation. Leadership is a skill that may start internally but manifests itself in the real world. Never lose sight of that fact. How you choose to lead and the example you set directly impacts your business and your team. If you are excited and energized, they will be too. If you are a defeatist, that will impact your team's performance.

The mental game becomes a real-world game very quickly. That is why it is important to understand how you impact others and why leadership is a practice and not a destination.

IT IS AN EVOLUTION

All things change through time. Leadership is no different.

While some timeless elements are universally applicable, much of what we do and practice is an evolution. We learn more; we evolve. We interact with new teams or business partners, we evolve. We experience a financial crisis or unforeseen event, we evolve.

Nothing stays static. We either improve or get worse, but we never stay the same. Leadership is an evolution of self, opinions, communication, and tools.

IT IS ABOUT SELF-DISCOVERY

Challenge brings growth. As you move through this journey, you will discover more about yourself than you ever imagined. As you change roles and grow in your career, you will approach similar situations with a different lens. Leadership is about being authentic, and to do that, you must take the time to understand who you really are and what matters to you. True leaders look in the mirror before they attempt to change others. You can't change others until you take a critical eye to yourself, your strengths, and your weaknesses. You can't change yourself and your habits if you don't take the time to discover them.

Solitude is critical. We have far too much noise in our world, and if we do not take time to tune it out regularly, we will find ourselves burned out, stressed out, crying out for help. I am not talking about 60 minutes of meditation, chanting, and scented candles, although if that is your thing, go nuts. I am talking about taking time for regularly scheduled breaks. Focus on the essentials in life, and don't be controlled by your calendar. Whether it is 10-15 minutes per day or a week in the summer, take time out with no email, no distraction, and just be. Go for a walk outside or just sit in a park. Enjoy the stillness and the quiet. Let your thoughts zigzag through your head and watch them go. Deliberately slow down and turn off the noise. This is a critical element in your leadership journey. Without it, you will be reacting and slowly overreacting. Quiet the mind and give yourself time and permission to refocus.

It is also about values. As you read this, think about your personal values. Do they align with where you are in your life or career? Values are those things that allow you to prioritize, focus on the essential, and provide guardrails that will not be crossed.

When used correctly, your core values lead to a strong foundation for leadership. While your values may vary, here are some common core values of successful leaders.

- Keep your word and be accountable for your actions
- Tell the truth (or at least don't lie)
- Don't give up
- Be hungry
- Find out – it is better knowing than not knowing
- Build a vision for your future - don't get stuck in the perceived past "glory days."
- Find your own voice and be authentic
- Be open to change and have a willingness to adapt – we either get better or worse but never stay the same
- Be a sponge – learn and implement
- Strive for excellence – chase it, never be satisfied but enjoy the process

IT IS ABOUT PROGRESSIVE IMPROVEMENT

This will not happen overnight. It takes time; that is why I call it a practice and a journey. You will not become a world-class leader overnight.

Speaking of that term...what the hell does that mean anyway? I am sure you have heard that term as well, and I can tell you, it is completely worthless.

Is there a standard measure of success in becoming a better leader?

Nope.

Does everyone lead the same way?

Nope.

Does everyone have the same background, education, and frame of reference?

Nope, nope, and nope.

Strive to improve and learn every day. Incremental improvements over time are sustainable and keep your ego in check. It is the little things that add up to the big successes. Those minor things you do every day, over time, move the big rocks. If you cannot achieve incremental improvement, you will unlikely achieve it with one big swing.

Be your best self, strive for greatness but look to take the best practices of leaders you admire and make them your own.

IT LASTS THE REST OF YOUR LIFE

Leadership is not a one and done thing, nor is it purely linked to your job title. It is a lifetime pursuit, a practice. Leadership skills will serve you in whatever role you have or wherever your life takes you. It doesn't end when you go home for the day or when you change roles; leadership is part of who you are.

PART 2

"A leader is someone who demonstrates what's possible."

-Mark Yarnell

A LEADER KNOWS HOW TO COMMUNICATE

Be clear about your expectations of others; leave nothing uncertain. Communication must be a two-way street, so encourage your team to be open and honest with you. Encourage them to deconstruct things to find out why they worked or didn't work. Communicate regularly and openly, allow the team to grow, fail, and to learn.

As a leader, you must create a safe environment for honesty, candor, and ease of communication. This is the foundation for building a high-performing team that feels comfortable challenging ideas, providing constructive feedback, and generating solutions that will drive the strategy and the business forward.

A LEADER KNOWS HOW TO HANG ON

Things will not always go your way. The world will not always like your ideas, and some days you will spill coffee on your pants. This is how it goes. Once we build momentum and get going, we cannot let obstacles and difficult days stop us. They may slow us down, but we will regroup and take what the day gives us only to fight again tomorrow.

There will be great days, and there will be awful days. Some days you will be flying, and other days are just hanging on. When it feels like you are barely hanging on, remember leaders know that everything can be used for a purpose.

A LEADER KNOWS HOW TO EMPOWER AND LET GO

A leader knows how to challenge their team (or themselves) to get to the next level of performance. Stretch them.

Build their skills.

Increase opportunities for visibility.

Rules for empowering others:

1. Don't try to do everything yourself or micromanage people.
2. Empower your team and allow them to find the best path forward (it will most likely be different from yours, and that is a good thing.)
3. Hold them accountable but get them to share their methodology for problem-solving – it is critical to understand how they dissect problems to better learn from mistakes and even wins.
4. Failure will happen; accept this, and then use it as a learning opportunity.

5. Learn from others – be open to ideas and solutions from all levels, departments, industries, and different frames of reference.

6. Infuse your team with the skills you lack. I cannot stress this enough – build a team that has complementary skills, not homogenous skills that become redundant over time.

A LEADER KNOWS HOW TO HOLD PEOPLE ACCOUNTABLE

Throughout my career, I have met with various teams in multiple businesses and industries. Whether it was for a project or just as a focus group, one of the recurring topics was centered on empowerment. As part of a team, most people want to be empowered to make decisions and use the expertise that they brought when they joined the company. Of course, not everyone craves this type of authority, but I think most people would prefer it over the alternative. While empowerment sounds great on the surface, there is another component that is required for success. That is, of course, accountability.

These two go together, but how do you instill a culture of empowerment and continuous improvement while holding people accountable?

It starts with a detailed strategy that is clearly communicated to all members of the team and then allows them to set their own goals and measures of success aligned with the larger strategy. Once that is done, it comes down to communication. As a leader, check-in regularly with your team and see how things are going. Give them the freedom to adjust if something changes or new information is received that will alter the strategy itself or the planned tactical response.

Empowerment = Accountability. You can't have one without other if you truly want a culture of high performance.

Involve people in making a process better or improving customer experience. It will allow them to use the skills they possess and help them feel like they are adding value beyond their daily tasks.

It is about ownership. They own the decision; there is no one to blame. Use it as a teaching moment, but the team must know the buck stops with them. By allowing people to make decisions, learn from mistakes and take ownership, you will find that most will not only rise to the occasion but will exceed your expectations if you give them a chance. This is where the skill of deconstruction comes into play. Encourage the team to deconstruct projects or initiatives, whether they worked or not, to better understand the thought process and to learn how to improve in the future. Many books talk about learning from failure and failing fast. Those points are important to remember; learning from failure can be better than a college education. However, don't lose sight of the fact that there is much to be learned in success as well as failure.

A LEADER KNOWS TO SPEED TRUMPS PERFECTION

Speed combined with hard work will trump anything. By focusing on speed, you are indirectly focusing on execution. Perfection is paralysis. If you wait for perfection, nothing will get accomplished. You will be standing still while your competition is running circles around you.

Be fast, deliver value to your clients every day. The big goals take time, but the day-to-day execution relies on speed, not perfection. Take the time to build a simple, scalable process but don't focus solely on perfection. Set yourself and your business up with a plan and then begin executing as soon as possible.

Strategy can be slow; you can and should take the time to develop it and communicate it. A good strategy takes time to build. The flip side of that is execution. Execution must be fast. The path must be clear for teams to travel but let them determine the tools they use and the means to accomplish the goal.

Execution should add value, be relentless in your pursuit of value creation. Don't waste time focusing on perfection at the expense of execution.

Execution drives your organization forward. To accomplish your goals, you will need speed.

A LEADER KNOWS HOW TO TAKE BIG SWINGS

Opportunities show up when you least expect them. Even the best leaders cannot anticipate every possible scenario, but they do have the ability to prepare for possibilities. To do this, you need to be realistic about your own processes, team, and skills. Despite our best efforts and metrics, processes don't age well. Take time to identify weaknesses and develop solutions or ways to mitigate those weaknesses. Enable your team to do their best work and trust their judgment in simplifying the process and workflow.

If you pursue a mindset of continuous improvement, simplification, and empowerment, you can be ready when an opportunity presents itself.

Don't be afraid to blow up a process and start over. Sometimes the easiest way forward is to go backward and start a new path.

A LEADER KNOWS HOW TO MANAGE RISK

If you're running a business that refuses to change and adapt as the world and the environment around it changes, you will find yourself with a much higher risk profile and a fast track to extinction.

Bold business leadership requires a tolerance for the right kinds of risk and accepting failure as an option. Most importantly, it requires a capacity to forge ahead in the wake of setbacks or even defeat. Tactics may change, but the strategy should remain if it still makes sense.

Healthy risk-taking requires coming to the table as educated and informed as possible about the path ahead. Proactively identify as much of the risk as possible and then look for ways to mitigate it. You will never remove the risk entirely, but you can reduce it to an acceptable level.

Remember the following points with respect to risk:

1. Anything that is new and different is inherently risky but critical to success
2. Weigh the pros and cons of each risk and know your level of tolerance
3. Learn from failures and adjust as needed. Don't let failure or mistakes control you and force you to withdraw or, worse, revert to the old way of doing things.

A LEADER KNOWS HOW TO PROJECT OPTIMISM

Every business will face its share of ups and downs. There will be difficulties and challenges regardless of industry or the best planning. There will be times when you will be unsure if you chose the correct direction. This is all normal; we are all human.

However, humans also crave the bright side of things. We are drawn to hope. As a leader, infuse some level of optimism into just about everything that you communicate and how you act. Optimism should be genuine but also grounded in reality. When projecting expectations for the future, learn to frame tough situations or setbacks as learning experiences. As we talked about a few pages ago, there is something to be learned in everything, whether success or failure.

People will notice, and their confidence will grow as a result. Sure, a strategy or initiative may not be successful, but a leader can chart a course forward that

guarantees personal and professional growth
regardless of the result.

A LEADER IS CURIOUS

Don't just assume the old way (or the current way) of doing things is the correct or the best way. Look around. Talk to people in other industries, read different perspectives. Challenge everything. Remember, there are many ways to do things and many perspectives on problem-solving. Look around corners and in obscure places to find new ways to simplify a process, reduce costs, connect better with people, or improve customer experience. It is all out there if you take the time to find it.

Sometimes being curious involves getting your hands dirty and diving into why things are done the way they are done, and then asking why. Take the time to meet and talk with the people who perform various tasks within your team and understand why the process is what it is. Then challenge them to find a better way.

Be curious.

Stay hungry and foolish.

Look beyond what is done now to how things could be done in the future.

Allow for continuous improvement and keep things simple.

A LEADER HAS A FUTURE FOCUS

No matter the industry, there is always room for improvement, and where there's room for improvement, there is always a potential for disruption.

Disruption is inevitable, so leaders must develop a future focus and be a bit of a futurist. Don't get stuck thinking about things as they are, but rather how they could be. Balance your focus between addressing the present needs of the market while also addressing what the market could look like in two, three, ten years from now.

Seek out opportunities, even in success, to wield the power of disruption yourself. It is not limited to small firms or start-ups. Be the disruptor, look around corners, and take time to see trends forming that can advance your team to the next level or even be ready when the market catches up.

To be successful at becoming a futurist, keep the following points in mind:

1. Be present while leading into the future – don't neglect the here and now while still thinking long-term.
2. Embrace disruption, and don't be afraid to disrupt yourself, your process, or your strategy.
3. Change is inevitable; either lead the way or find your future controlled by others.
4. Shape the future – continuously experiment and learn rapidly. Find new ways of working, learn from failure, simplify.
5. Build a future-focused team and culture (skills, beliefs, values, etc.)
6. Encourage your team to be intellectually curious, open to change, resilient, and flexible.

Leaders should be fascinated and energized by the future. As a leader, you shouldn't be satisfied with the status quo, rather look for ways to go beyond 'what is' to 'what could be.' Great leaders strive to inspire their teams to make a better future a reality; this is leadership.

A LEADER KNOWS HOW TO ADD VALUE

Traditionally the focus of leaders has been to maximize value to shareholders. Today, leaders need a new approach to create meaningful value for all stakeholders. To create sustainable value beyond the next quarter, we need to add value to our customers, employees, partners, and the community, in addition to the stockholders. Adding value means going beyond the pre-set expectations. It is driving the organization forward.

By changing the frame of reference, we can create a more open system of contribution and a larger pool of value-focused teams. To do this, leaders must build a compelling purpose and vision. It must be the "True North" that is clear to the organization, its customers, its shareholders, and even suppliers.

To achieve this, leaders must create open and empowered organizations that are able to continually plan, execute and adjust resources as priorities or business conditions change.

Leaders also need to act as a coach. They need to develop their team beyond just performance. A leader should work with their team to fully develop the proper mindset, enhance skills and domain knowledge, just like in sports. As teams become more empowered, they will need more coaching and less direct "managing" as they think strategically, collaborate deeply, and deconstruct problems or processes to find solutions.

Finally, leaders need to be energetic and project that energy to their team and their customers. Energy is contagious. Everyone can feel the difference when you encounter a high-energy person versus a low-energy person. By projecting, energy and enthusiasm help the teamwork in an energetic yet sustainable way. Additionally, leaders need to foster connections and partnerships at all levels of the organization, remove roadblocks, and help people connect what they do with the larger strategy. They need to see how what they do adds direct or indirect value to the organization and its stakeholders. This helps build a sense of ownership which allows them to see the bigger picture while reinforcing the need for empowerment.

This is a shift to how many leaders have always operated. By looking at value through a new lens, leaders can unleash the passion and potential of their team. This approach leads to a much more sustainable path to deliver results and continually add value to a diverse set of stakeholders.

A LEADER NEVER STOPS LEARNING

Always grow and extract wisdom from what you have done, both good and bad. Keep learning and expand your frame of reference. It may expand and veer off in unexpected directions, but learning should never stop.

Life will teach you humility. Learn to figure out why things worked or don't work. As I have said a few times now, take time to learn from successes _and_ failures, don't allow either to prevent forward progress. Take time for self-reflection and self-discipline.

Self-discipline is very important; you need to be mindful of and control your unproductive emotions. Not only is this good for mental health and managing stress, but it helps to reinforce the mindset and culture you want for your team.

Control what you can, and don't allow the rest to overwhelm you. It sounds easy to say, but we cannot control many things in our life, yet we allow them to ruin our day, week, or year. Focus on what you can control and build from there. When you think about how little you truly control, it is almost liberating.

Control what you read or choose to learn.

Control your anger.

Control your response.

Control how you spend your time.

Hone your listening skills.

Practice empathy.

It is impossible to know everything. In the ever-changing modern world, it is easy to get out of date real fast. Put your ego aside, take time to learn, and even embrace becoming a beginner again once in a while. It will reboot your frame of reference and allow you to view things through a fresh lens.

A LEADER NEVER FORGETS WHERE THEY CAME FROM

None of us started at the top. We all started at an entry point at some time in our careers. Never forget that. Remember that others are on their own journey and may just be starting where you once stood.

Empathize with that point of view. A leader should have high expectations and see the potential in people but, at the same time, remember all of us have different backgrounds and different learning curves. Don't expect people who are new to have all the answers but provide the guidance to get them past the entry point and to the next level.

All of us have relied on someone (or several people) throughout our careers to help get us on the right path, and no one can go it alone. As a leader, never forget that. Remember what it is like to be new or to be inexperienced and learning and then use that to help them on their journey.

Every one of us has an origin story. We have started our professional careers in some way, made mistakes, learned from them, and had people take chances on us. Learn from that experience and use it as a foundation for empathy and to keep your ego in check. None of us is as good as we think we are.

PART 3

"Our chief want is someone who will inspire us to be what
we know we could be."

-Ralph Waldo Emerson

A LEADER IS INTERESTED IN THEIR TEAM

A good leader knows as much about their team as they do their numbers. Now, you can dispute this, but without creating a personal connection with your team, sustained excellence is not possible. Without sustained excellence, numbers become much harder to attain consistently.

Leadership is not just about you. It is about your team, your organization, and your customers. Take care of them, and you will be amazed at how easy numbers become.

Engage with people in an informal way. Walk around and talk to people. Be interested in your team, and I mean genuinely interested. Please get to know them and what motivates them. Learn their strengths and the details of their background or experience. This will help you as you take on new challenges allowing you to better play to your strengths as a team.

Build awareness of other people and demonstrate empathy. As you build relationships with your team and with others, take time to view things from another's point of view.

A LEADER INSPIRES

Leaders are only leaders because they inspire others to follow them. Now, you can say, "well, I am a VP; people have to listen to what I say." Well, technically, that is true. But, how long can you stay in that role if you have underperforming teams and high turnover? Not long.

Inspire people to follow you or want to join your team.

Create an environment for them to learn, take chances, and grow.

Make it ok (and safe) to fail.

Inspire people to take risks.

People don't want to be "managed." They want to be part of something bigger, to be valued for what they do, and make a difference. Leaders believe in people and inspire them to achieve more than they thought possible. Allow room for failure and course correct if needed but give your team room to problem solve. Allow them room to move and act based on their assessment of the situation. If they are correct, celebrate the win. If not, reflect on what could have been done differently.

Always seek to understand their thought process. This is critical for reinforcing or adjusting for the future. This will only further enhance their problem-solving skills.

Be curious. Look around corners and see opportunities that others may not see, then inspire people to make them a reality.

A LEADER LEARNS FROM FAILURE

Failure is a powerful teacher. Just like a bad boss can teach you more about leadership (or lack thereof) than a good one, it is ok to fail.

Learn from it.

Embrace it.

Articulate why you took the path you did and expect the same from your team. The thought process is critical here – if you can deconstruct a decision, then you can better absorb the lesson. You and the team can see where to adjust in the future.

Failure brings growth and will teach you more than a year's worth of training if you take the time to deconstruct it and learn from it.

A LEADER CREATES ONE VISION

To be successful, you need to create a single-minded pursuit of excellence through the team's culture. As we discussed in the previous section, this is your "true north." Infuse the team with energy and passion for winning by providing context, meaning, and consistent expectations. Successful leaders create broad-based cultural expectations for performance. Everyone knows what is accepted and expected as well as what won't be tolerated.

When setting priorities, try to limit to three. Any more than that, and their focus will be too broad. As a leader, you must articulate priorities very effectively and repeatedly. This is not because people don't get it; you just need to reinforce what is important in a world full of noise. There are many distractions; regular communication and reinforcement of priorities will help drive execution on the things that matter.

As you establish and communicate the strategy, be sure to collect feedback through regular touchpoints with your team. This is critical to not only reinforce priorities but to allow your team to own the vision. Build a culture where performance is expected and where honesty and candor are encouraged.

Remember, a strategy and the critical priorities to achieve it are only as good as your ability to articulate them to the team.

A LEADER CREATES ONE UNIFIED, YET DIVERSE TEAM

Earlier I wrote about empowerment and accountability. There is a clear connection between those two elements and peak performance. However, it starts long before you assign a task. It starts at the time of the team formation.

To build a successful and high-performing team, a leader needs to build complementary skillsets and go beyond the traditional background of a specific job. For example, hiring someone with a background in psychology could be extremely valuable in cybersecurity, even if they have never written a line of code in their life. Yes, credentials and skills matter, but attitude matters more. Most things can be taught, but attitude is hard to change. Identify core attributes that you need from your team to be successful and then build around those. Look for complementary skills that also reinforce your weak points. Pay attention to how the team interacts with one another and with other teams, provide coaching and guidance, and always make sure the balance you want is present.

A LEADER BUILDS ON INTANGIBLES

You can't learn everything about a person from their CV. They are the culmination of their education, experience, training, and development as a human. Leaders must understand this to not only build a high-performing team but to learn how to play to strengths. Every one of us brings certain intangibles to our jobs. Skills that are just below the surface may not be easily noticed or detected, but they will play a crucial role in long-term success if they can be brought to the surface and developed.

Look beyond what you see, find out what each person brings to the table, and help them draw on that to go to levels they never thought possible while bringing the rest of the team along for the ride.

A LEADER WILL PLAY TO STRENGTHS

Challenge people and allow them to grow but also play to your strengths and the strengths of your team. Allow people to spend time in their comfort zone and deepen those skills. It will help reinforce confidence but also continue to build the bench strength that many organizations lack.

Remember, this is about setting your team up for success. Everything is balance. Trust your team and the skills they bring; leverage their expertise when needed. Find the right balance for your team and organization. Focus your efforts around what your team needs to learn and what they want to learn, or how they want to grow. You will not only keep them motivated to grow, but you will foster the spirit of continuous improvement by knowing where people's strengths lie and what they want to learn.

A LEADER LEARNS FROM BAD BOSSES (PAST & PRESENT)

We have all had "bad" bosses in our careers. In some cases, we notice it immediately, and other times it becomes apparent over time. Most people default to one of two behaviors. Either they try to outlast their boss on their team/department, or they not so secretly hope others will notice and take action to remove them, or maybe the boss will just move on to a new role somewhere. The other option, probably the most common, is the employee starts to look for a new job.

The problem with the first option is it relies on stamina and hope. Hope will not last and is not a strategy. Neither are overly productive but are the most common. I would suggest a third option. Learn from them.

It sounds crazy but takes the time to observe and sometimes endure. Of course, I am not suggesting you stay in a toxic role for the sake of an experiment. But, even in the middle of a job search, you can use the mental notes to make sure you don't jump from one bad situation to another or, more importantly, use that data to become a better leader yourself.

Bad bosses exist in every company, and everyone has had at least one in their career. However, you can still learn from them. Use the experience for all that it is worth, even if all you learn is how NOT to act toward your team and others in the organization.

Sometimes, all you can do is use it as a learning experience and become a better leader as a result.

A LEADER BUILDS A HIGH-PERFORMING TEAM

Every team has a story. Some have been together for years, while others have been recently formed. Some are co-located, while other teams are completely virtual. Regardless of the location or the length of service, teams that function at a high level stand out add value consistently, and set the standard for other teams to follow.

But how do you form a high-performing team or, more to the point, how do you take a low-performing team and turn them into a high-performance group? How do you build on personal strengths and empower people to forge their own path while actively executing the corporate strategy? Building high-performing teams are not impossible, and it just takes the right mindset and an ability to see beyond a resume.

Let's begin at the beginning...assembling a high-performing team from scratch.

Critical variables include but are not limited to experience, humor, personality, and strategic thinking. These variables are not all-inclusive, but I have found them to be the perfect blend in assembling a high-performing team. As we move forward in the process, let's walk through each of the critical success factors and understand why they are important to the team dynamic.

> **Experience:** this is the easiest one of them all but is often misused. All too often, companies are looking for specialists in a field with years of experience derived from repetition. It is counterintuitive, but that is detrimental to team chemistry. The exact opposite builds the foundation you need for a high-performing team. The beauty of a generalist is twofold. First, they can plug and play in multiple areas, which is very useful to small businesses and growing companies. Second, they provide an outsider's perspective that allows you to

proactively identify process breakdowns and areas of improvement because they are more readily able to ask "why." They have no interest in maintaining the status quo because they are not part of the status quo.

Humor: one of the most critical elements of a high-performing team. Projects, sales quotas, and deadlines can impact chemistry and add unnecessary stress. Having people on the team that know the importance of their contribution but are willing to make mistakes and laugh at themselves is an undervalued characteristic. Teams bond with humor. They release stress through humor. They hold each other accountable but in a way that increases comfort rather than competition within the team.

Personality: Like humor, personality is a critical element in high-performing teams. Personality has two components. First is the obvious one...the personality of the individual team members. The second component, the team personality, is again often overlooked. As the team begins to gel and bond, a team personality forms where people feed off the energy and drive of the others on the team. They begin to excel because they don't want to let their teammates down. It is critical when expanding the team that the leader understands this relationship and looks to add people that will fit in the group dynamic while possessing the right individual attitude coming into the team.

Strategic Thinking: Arguably the most important component of high-performing teams, but probably the most forgotten in many companies. It is critical to provide the strategic roadmap of where the team and/or business is going over the next 3-5 years. Without a clear destination in mind, there is about a 99% chance you will never get there. The sad truth is this is exactly where teams fail in many companies. They may have goals or sales targets for the month or quarter but no real strategic roadmap beyond the short-term.

Without this critical component, teams are set up to fail without even knowing it. I used to work at a company that had a Director of Strategy (as many firms do). He was arguably the least strategic Director of Strategy you could imagine. Not only could he not see market conditions changing or business trends emerging, but he also would never wait long enough to let an initiative play out. He would abruptly change things for change's sake or bring in more consultants to "optimize" the process.

On top of that, he not only didn't seem to believe that his team was as smart as he was. That led to continuously changing direction mid-stream and ignoring advice from both consultants and senior team members. This resulted in ineffectiveness, continuous change without improvement, and frustrated employees. Sufficed to say, this was not a recipe for success. I'd like to say that the executive team caught on to this and replaced this guy, but unfortunately, bad leadership was compounded by absentee leadership at the executive level.

The bottom line is this...

If you hire the best talent, provide the roadmap, and then empower them to chart the course to the destination, you will build a high-performing team in the long term. Empowerment, accountability & team chemistry are the foundation for long-lasting, high-performing teams. Allow your team to demonstrate their skillset and add value to your business. If you don't, you are likely to lose your top performers to a company that will allow them to add value to *their* organization.

A LEADER MAKES INFORMED DECISIONS

Decision-making is critical for a leader. Often, you will be relying on imperfect information, unrealistic deadlines, limited upside, or all the above. The key is to make informed decisions that you can revisit later for a lesson learned. Remember that you can always learn from something, whether it worked or not.

To improve your decision making, think about the following concepts:

1. Make the best decisions you can with the information that you have
2. Depend on your team, leverage their expertise
3. Ask for perspective and listen to your team, but remember you are accountable for the final decision – no passing the buck
4. Stay up to date on trends and issues in your industry and others; there may be some knowledge you can leverage

5. Hear all sides and quickly weigh options before deciding
6. Weigh the pros and cons of each option, but don't use procrastination as an excuse to avoid making the decision. Review options and the impact of those options quickly and succinctly
7. Own your decision

Whatever you do, <u>be decisive</u>. Yes, make decisions carefully and thoughtfully but become a leader who can make decisions efficiently and definitively. Once you decide – stick with it. Accept failure and consequences as an opportunity for growth and move on.

A LEADER LEARNS HOW TO HANDLE PRAISE

You are never as good as people tell you. Everyone likes to hear praise and feel appreciated. Where many people go wrong is, they allow that one achievement, that one moment to satisfy them. Don't do that.

Stay hungry, never be satisfied. Appreciate the wins, be cordial to people who praise you, and then get back to work. We only get better or worse; we never stay the same.

Praise is fleeting, but hard work and diligence to your craft ensure. Let the process be the reward. Enjoy the moments, but then let them pass and get back to the things that got you to that place and to that positive feedback.

A LEADER LEARNS HOW TO HANDLE PANIC

Make no mistake about it, crises will occur, and you will see your fair share of challenges. As a leader, people are looking to you to solve the problem and provide assurance that everything will work out. This is not about providing a delusional response but rather providing clarity to a difficult situation.

The key is knowing and accepting those bad things that happen unexpectedly. Start by planning in advance with your team. Don't try to plan for every possible scenario but do think about what is most critical to your business and then think of ways those critical processes or teams could be impacted. Know your risks and make sure you have the right people in the room.

Planning for a crisis or disaster recovery should not be done in a vacuum but should be part of a much larger cross-functional effort. Surround yourself with the right people, document your plan and communicate it thoroughly. This won't stop a crisis from happening, but it will allow your team and your business the chance to react properly when it does and recover much faster. That is leadership...looking around the corner, seeing what is coming, and then planning accordingly.

A LEADER LEARNS HOW TO PROVIDE FEEDBACK

Regular feedback is critical for a productive, engaged team. No one should be surprised at annual review time for good or bad. That is a bad practice that occurs far too often in too many companies.

Timely feedback serves two key purposes. First, it creates cohesion between the leader and the team. It also helps reinforce things that should be in focus and prioritized. Second, it is a launchpad for personal growth to foster a mindset of continuous improvement and deconstructing failures. This is a critical skill that most people need time and proper coaching to develop.

Giving your team regular updates on personal performance along with information on the overall business helps them feel both valued and connected. While all feedback is not necessarily positive, all feedback can serve a purpose to help someone course correct or simply learn a new way to approach a problem or a situation. A side benefit is that regular touchpoints also build rapport with your team.

Leaders must provide feedback that is both timely and constructive. Don't wait to reinforce strengths or course-correct development needs until annual review time. You will lose people due to uncertainty by the time the next review cycle starts. Regular feedback creates a culture of trust, candor, and respect. Think about a feedback structure that you valued as you were rising in your career or that a mentor used. Use that as a starting point. It won't be perfect, but like everything else will require time and thought to ensure the best fit for your team.

Everyone on your team may want or need different levels of feedback and connection. Customize based on the needs of your team and adjust as needed. Regardless of how you implement, start with a consistent framework for regular discussions like quarterly goal reviews and weekly/bi-weekly one-on-ones. Once you have a basic structure in place, you can adjust from there based on feedback from the team. If you schedule one-on-one sessions, let them drive the conversation. Make the meeting about them and not just a shorter version of the larger team meeting.

PART 4

"*A good leader inspires others with confidence in him; a great leader inspires them with confidence in themselves.*"

-Unknown

BUILDING FOCUS, STRATEGY, AND PRIORITIES

As a leader, you need to provide the overarching strategy for your company, team, or department. Far too often, many people try to take on too much to make their goals look good for the year or simply because they feel they must.

The truth is you can only truly focus on three or four priorities at a time. Any more than that and your focus will drift from one task to another, and overall performance will suffer. Of course, these priorities can change based on business conditions, but they need to be simple and focused. Less is more.

Take time monthly or quarterly to re-evaluate priorities to make sure you are still working on the right things. If you need to adjust, do it. It not, keep executing.

Regularly articulate priorities to your team. Be candid and guide them where needed. The team's priorities should never be in doubt. If they are unclear, team execution will suffer, and you will find yourself dealing with subpar results. A strategy is only as good as your ability to articulate, prioritize, and execute it.

BUILDING EXECUTION INTO STRATEGY

For a strategic change to be effective, you must be able to execute. If you can't execute it, the change is nothing more than words on the page or PowerPoint. If it is a personal change, you must be committed every day to make the change through small, incremental improvements. If the change is part of your strategy, you need to build trust and commitment on a larger scale. Far too often, strategic discussions are limited to the executive team or senior management, and it barely makes it to the team doing the work. That is a critical miss in planning as well as a missed opportunity. Of course, this doesn't mean that you should broadcast every strategic decision or plan to all levels of the organization. Rather, it means that you should build execution into your strategy, and execution involves the people who are tasked with implementation and beyond.

Inspire your team with a strategic vision. Inspire them to feel a part of it, to own the outcome, and to add value to it. To minimize the risk of distrust or lack of enthusiasm, engage your people on the front lines, those who must execute the strategy every day. They are the ones with the process expertise and are also closest to your customers. If they are removed from the process, or things are hidden that impact the day-to-day operations, the strategy will become ineffective over time because it lacks the linkage to how things really operate. This is the linkage that the team working in and with the process can provide.

Through this engagement, you will link your team to the solution and thus fulfill a basic human need for recognition. This allows your team to feel a part of the strategy, to own it, and make it succeed. This is also how you create trust, commitment, and cooperation long after the strategy is in place. Your team should not be measured by their hierarchical value but rather by the value that they contribute to the organization.

CONNECT STRATEGY TO WHAT PEOPLE DO EVERY DAY

Don't build a self-licking ice cream cone.

Strategy is only good when people can link it to what they do every day. If it isn't part of what the business does today, find out why before building a plan. This sounds silly and rather basic, but you would be amazed (or maybe not) at the number of times this happens in organizations.

Be curious and ask questions. Take the time to find out why things are the way they are, and then empower your team to fix something that isn't working. Understand what they do and ask them if they would do it that way if it were their business. This is invaluable to learning where holes are in the process or potential points of failure.

Connect with people on the larger responsibility to create value and not just do things one way because "it's always been done that way." Engage people to think differently, to view the process or their job as if it were their company to drive ownership and create a new mindset for change.

ALLOW YOUR TEAM TO DEVELOP THE TACTICS THAT FULFILL THE STRATEGY

To drive an increased level of ownership on your team, provide the overall strategy and then step back and let them map the road to achieving that strategy. If you have built a strong team, let them surprise you with their ingenuity.

Provide guidance to keep them on the rails but let them decide the tactics. In most companies, the people doing the job every day will know more about what works and what doesn't than the executive team. Leverage that experience to build a strong process and an even stronger path to executing your vision.

INFLUENCING CHANGE

No one really likes to change, especially when that change impacts what they do every day or have grown comfortable with. Typically, people embrace it under one of two circumstances. First, when it aligns to something that we need or want more, something beyond the status quo. It must link to or provide a path forward to more growth, productivity, or revenue with less risk. There must be some benefit to the other person.

The other side of the coin is less pleasant. If change doesn't align with our present goals or needs, humans tend to embrace it when they have no other option. When it is the last best choice, it becomes a need.

The key to influencing change is to align the why behind the project to the needs of the impacted business teams or functions. They do not care about charters or project plans, or schedules. They care about adding value, increasing income and productivity while decreasing risk. If you can connect the project why to the needs of those that you need to make it successful, you will win their support and, in the end, drive long-lasting change. Understand the teams and roles that are impacted by your project and how that change will impact them. This is less about influencing and more about knowing your audience and targeting your efforts rather than treating everyone the same. That is how most people approach a political hurdle, and then they wonder why it didn't work. To ensure you break down political barriers and build the right coalition, you need to know the following:

1. Who are the stakeholders?
2. Who will fight me?
3. Who has the most to lose with a change to the status quo?
4. Who are my supporters?
5. Who will naturally align with this initiative and support it?

6. Who has the most to gain from this strategic change?

Identify your supporters and detractors. Ignore everyone in the middle at this point. Move quickly to communicate with your various groups and create a win-win scenario as best you can. Understand their perceived pain points and anticipate their objections. If you cannot bring resolution to their objections, isolate your detractors by building a broader coalition of support while addressing their key objections. The key to winning over your detractors is to know their likely angles of attack early and build counterpoints supported by your coalition and backed by data and reason. Once you do that, you will reduce the risk of a political war before it even begins.

PART 5

"Become the kind of leader that people would follow voluntarily, even if you have no title or position."

-Brian Tracy

LEADERSHIP IS NOT ABOUT YOU

Leadership is all about other people and bringing out their best while getting them to achieve things that they never thought possible. You are a leader because people follow you, period.

If you think you are a leader only because of your title, you will not remain that for very long.

Three Commandments for becoming a better leader:

1. Treat people how you would like to be treated by your boss
2. Give them opportunities to grow and add value beyond their day to day activities
3. Help them to become the best version of themselves. They cannot be your clone, so stop trying to make them an alternate version of you.

LEADERSHIP IS A CHOICE

You do not need a title or rank to be a leader. Leaders come from all walks of life, and experience may vary.

Be good at helping people.

Take ownership of your decisions.

Build trust and lead by example.

Be the person that can get things done and that people see as a problem solver.

BE GOOD AT HELPING PEOPLE

Be good at helping people, both inside and outside your team. Model the behavior you want your team to have.

Learn to be the last to speak and thoughtfully listen. Far too many people are so busy thinking about what they are going to say next that they fail to hear what someone else is saying. To be good at helping people, you first need to know what they need help with...then you can act. Sounds simple, but I had seen many people try to "help" when there was nothing wrong, or they didn't even know the problem.

When you are meeting with someone, simply sit there and take it all in. Ask questions, check for understanding, and don't rush to a solution. You will find that sometimes, EQ is more important than IQ. Spend more time listening and less time talking. Don't merely nod and use the time to think of your response; truly listen.

Practice being the last to speak.

Be humble.

Take it all in and be present.

LEAD BY EXAMPLE

Leadership only succeeds when it shows others how to extend and push for greatness beyond what they think they can do. Your team should look at you and how you work and then think, "if they can do it, so can I."

Demonstrate the behavior and the mindset that you want to see in your team. Get your hands dirty and spend some time in the trenches. This will allow you to see things from a new perspective but will also build morale with your team. Of course, I am not saying you spend hours and hours doing your team's job but stay close enough to be connected to reality.

As challenges arise (and they will), look for solutions and opportunities, not just desperate problems. Challenge the status quo and establish a baseline of excellence, a roadmap for the team to follow. Be clear about what constitutes success and what is expected, and then model that behavior every day.

Leading by example is the fastest way to train and develop a team. It also builds some street cred since your team will see that you are willing to get in there, and you can empathize with what they do all the time. When you as the leader hold yourself to a high standard and a high level of performance, your team will strive to do the same.

BE AUTHENTIC

Be a genuine person. Don't be something you're not just to appear successful or aggressive or whatever. Like your mom probably told you at one point when you were a kid, just be yourself. Have genuine empathy for people and acknowledge when you don't know something.

Care about people.

Take a genuine interest in them, and don't be afraid to give them the chance to take a genuine interest in you.

If you don't know something, that's ok. Leaders don't get paid to know everything. They get paid to know where to get answers, empower people to get answers and assemble the people who get things done.

Be yourself. Be the person you were before people told you who to be.

RELAX AND RECHARGE

In the 21st century, we are always connected to a device or notification. Far too many people never give themselves enough time to completely disconnect and find some solitude to think or simply relax. It is critical to find downtime and stillness in your routine, not just once or twice a year on a half-assed vacation where you spent half the time reading email and aggravating your spouse by doing so. Leaders face incredible pressure and a pace that cannot be sustained indefinitely. Energy is not infinite.

The former CEO of Disney, Bob Iger, provided some insight into this concept, saying that "stillness was a critical element for planning." If you take the time for solitude to recharge, you can better focus on the bigger picture. Less work often means better work.

Some tips for making time to relax and recharge:

1. End your day by doing something pleasant and enriching that is not directly work-related – like

reading, journaling, listening to music, or even just watching a movie.

2. Unwind with exercise. It amazes me how many successful people are quite unsuccessful when it comes to their health and wellness. It is all part of the puzzle; if one is out of place, the picture is incomplete. Get outside, lift weights, go for a walk, anything to break a sweat.

3. Be social. Make time to connect and reconnect with people. This is especially important as our personal and professional responsibilities increase, and we need to make time to connect back with people and stay social.

4. Don't deplete your energy. Stop just short and take a break. For example, after working on something that requires deep concentration, take a 15-minute break to get coffee or tea or simply stretch or go for a little walk. You will be amazed at how much that works.

5. Give yourself time to think. Turn off the computer, no social media, just think. Let your mind run wild. Watch the ideas come and go and just be for a moment. Try to do this at least 10-minutes daily.

6. Find a place of respite. For me, this is the golf course or a hiking trail, or even my yard. Find a place you can go to read, think, or simply be alone with your thoughts. If inside, make the space yours with your favorite art, colors, or plants. It sounds loony, but it works.

7. Set boundaries for downtime and KEEP THEM! Personally, I like the early morning hours between 4:30 am, and 6 am. This is my time to focus, recharge, and think.

8. Balance your personal life with your work life. Take time to do fun things, spend time with your family, friends, and spouse. Take REAL vacations with no email or work, just time together.

9. Understand how you work and make sure you build in time for play. Remember as a kid you spent most of your days playing? There is no rule that says you cannot do that as an adult. All that changes is what you choose to do with your time.

10. Time is the most precious commodity that we have. We only get so much of it, and we can't get time back. It is a savings account that can only be drawn down; you cannot add more later. Spend it wisely and give yourself time to recharge. Work will always be waiting.

Remember that less work often means better work. Give yourself permission to relax, disengage and wander a bit. Some of my best work has come when I have paused for a time and then returned with a renewed perspective.

LEADERSHIP LESSONS

To be successful over the course of your career and as a leader, you will need to rely on other people. Leaders lead by example. They are watched far more than they realize and could become better leaders and mentors of future leaders just through their example.

In speaking with mentors and leaders that I admire over the course of my own journey, I have found the following to be core beliefs from successful leaders.

1. Communicate honestly with your team
2. Treat people with dignity and respect
3. Share credit AND responsibility
4. Build trust by keeping your word
5. Be consistent. If the situation changes, you should explain what changed and the impact on the team or the decision.
6. Give your team room to fail. Wrong steps lead to breakthroughs.

7. It is ok to take risks as long as you learn from them.
8. Give each person on the team individual attention. If you find that you cannot do that, look at your organization and your calendar to find out why.
9. Manage team conflict effectively, build the culture you need and then reinforce it.
10. Know when to let people go. Of course, you want everyone to succeed, but sometimes it just isn't a fit (see #9).
11. Set the right tone and let by example.
12. Respect others ALWAYS.
13. Provide timely inspiration, feedback, and praise.
14. Welcome open dialogue and different viewpoints.
15. Know when to promote, delegate, or increase responsibility.

TENETS FOR SUCCESS

Leadership is a very personal practice. What works for one may not work for another. That said, there are some best practices to keep in mind as you build your leadership practice.

1. Focus and consistency are imperative for strong leadership.
2. Define, share, and reinforce your strategic priorities regularly.
3. Involve your team in the strategic process, get their feedback and allow them room to run.
4. Empower people to execute the strategy tactically.
5. Hold people accountable but give them room to fail.
6. Clarity is an essential ingredient for leadership.
7. Evolve and adapt as the environment changes. If you are not getting better, you are getting worse

8. Take giant swings and set big goals to drive the business forward and allow your team room for growth.
9. Leadership is not about you – to be a leader, you need people that are willing to follow you
10. Be clear about your expectations of others – your team should always know where they stand and how success is measured

LEADERS NEED MENTORS TOO

Many successful people look for mentors as they begin and advance their careers, but then they reach their goal and then stop looking for advice. They feel as if they've arrived, reached the goal, climbed the mountain. They have seen it all, experienced it all, and have amassed significant knowledge along the way. That is the ego talking, and it is incredibly dangerous to continued improvement and growth.

Mentors can be both formal and informal. Informal mentoring can occur through books, podcasts, or other media. Informal mentoring is underappreciated. While formal, in-person mentors provide a strong reinforcement, informal mentors can provide a wide range of perspectives in a way that we could never take advantage of through a formal relationship. Plus, informal mentors can be living or dead!

Take time to explore new books, podcasts, and perspectives. Look beyond your industry or your expanded network to refresh your frame of reference and learn from a wide range of people. It will guaranty your growth and allow you to adjust your own frame of reference continuously.

We all get better or worse over time. None of us stays the same. If we do not expand our frame of reference and gain exposure to new ways of thinking, we will get worse, our skills will erode, and we will find ourselves trapped by ego.

Explore new ways of thinking, of approaching problems, and recharging. Look for people that continue to grow, excel, and thrive rather than those that become satisfied. Satisfaction is the enemy of greatness. To be a great leader, you must always strive to become better, to adapt to new ideas, to learn from others.

Look for mentors beyond your industry. Find them in books and music, and podcasts. Real relationships are important, but there is so much to be learned from successful people far beyond our personal network.

THE LEADERSHIP CANON

Leaders read and continuously learn. In fact, most successful people read 50+ books per year. While it doesn't matter how you consume the information (eBook, audiobook, or hardcover), what really matters is that you continue growing, learning, and building your toolkit as part of your practice.

This is a point in time list. There will be many others that are added, but here are some of my favorites to get you started:

1. The Art of War by Sun Tzu
2. CEO Material by D.A. Benton
3. The Rules of Work by Richard Templar
4. Start with Why by Simon Sinek
5. The McKinsey Way by Ethan Rasiel
6. Quirky by Melissa A. Schilling
7. How to Win Friends and Influence People by Dale Carnegie
8. Ego is the Enemy by Ryan Holiday

9. Tim Cook by Leander Kahney

10. Shoe Dog by Phil Knight

11. Linchpin by Seth Godin

12. Power by Jeffery Pfeffer

13. Principles by Ray Dalio

14. The Outsiders: Eight Unconventional CEOs and Their Radically Rational Blueprint for Success by William Thorndike

15. Unbeatable Mind by Mark Divine

16. The War of Art by Steven Pressfield*

*This is my most gifted book. We all face Resistance every day, time to learn what it is and how to beat it.

LEADERSHIP IS A PRACTICE

You will never be perfect but you can strive to get better every day. This is a journey, and your leadership style, tactics, beliefs, and methodology will evolve into the summation of all the information that you have absorbed. Never stop learning, never stop improving. Leadership is not something that can be mastered but rather only practiced.

Here is a recap of a few leadership lessons I hope you picked up in this short book:

1. Be curious – this is vital to being successful long term
2. Practice integrity in everything
3. Be honest and authentic
4. Strive for perfection, but really focus on execution
5. Be fair and give space for failure
6. Take responsibility for your own mistakes or poor decisions

7. Know when a decision needs to be made, act quickly and own it

8. Create a safe environment for honesty, candor, and failure

9. Be optimistic and believe in people – this will inspire your team and lead them far beyond where they thought they could go

10. Take time to relax and recharge – get away from the noise and let the stillness refresh you

Remember this is a journey, your journey. Enjoy it. Always continue to learn, to grow, and to improve. The journey never stops.

"Leadership and learning are indispensable to each other."

-John F. Kennedy

www.ingramcontent.com/pod-product-compliance
Lightning Source LLC
Chambersburg PA
CBHW030658220526
45463CB00005B/1829